The Chav
Guide to Life

LEE BOK

Crombie Jardine
PUBLISHING LIMITED

13 Nonsuch Walk, Cheam, Surrey, SM2 7LG
www.crombiejardine.com

Published by Crombie Jardine Publishing Limited
First edition, 2006

ISBN 1-905102-33-X

Designed by www.glensaville.com
Cover illustration by Helen West
Illustrations by Helen West, Rob Smith and www.glensaville.com
Printed and bound in Great Britain by
William Clowes Ltd, Beccles, Suffolk

THE CHAV GUIDE TO LIFE

The Meaning of 'Chav' p.5
Gear p.26
Jewellery and Accessories p.30
Names p.36
Language p.43
Lifestyle: Likes and Dislikes p.99
Food and Drink p.109
Jokes p.112
Chav Horoscopes p.122
Chav Icons: Top 10 Countdown . . p.135
The Chav Prayer p.150

The Meaning of 'Chav'

What does 'Chav' mean?

Chav is an insulting slang term now common throughout England. It is used to express a low opinion or negative criticism of someone. Generally speaking, it refers to a social group seen as uneducated, uncultured and likely to behave in an anti-social or dishonest way. The term Chav more often than not is applied to teenagers and young adults of white working-class or lower middle-class backgrounds.

Chav is used for both sexes, but sometimes a male is called a Chavster or a Chavo and a female a Chavette. There are many regional and local names that mean the same thing as Chav. Depending on where you happen to be in the country, they include Pikey, Townie, Bam, Barry, Bazza, Chaddite, Charver, Chavalier, Chavette, Chavster, Dumbo, Gazza, Hood Rat, Janner, Kev, Knacker, Ned, Ratboy, Rudeboy, Rudie, Scally, Schemie, Scutter, Shazza, Spide (Northern Ireland), Steek, Stig, Yarco, and Hatchy. In South Wales the words Townies and Scallies are used and are again associated with those wearing (presumably fake) Burberry clothing. In Scotland a male Chav is known as a Ned, whilst a female is known as a Nedette or (generally in the case of an older female Ned) a Senga.

The term Chav was first made popular in 2004 by the Popbitch website and was eagerly taken up by the tabloid press in the UK. Similar terms are used overseas when referring to a group of people sharing some of the same characteristics as Chavs: in the United States you have White Trash, Wigger or Nigger; in Australia the equivalent is Bogan; in Auckland, New Zealand, a common term is Westie. Nearer to home, in Ireland (especially Dublin) you have Scumbag and Scanger.

Some people shrug and accept the Chav term or label, but others do not like it, saying that it is a form of snobbery and serves no purpose other than to make fun of the lower classes.

Where does the term Chav come from?

So where does the word Chav come from? Well, there are many theories, some of which are:

1) The actual word Chav is commonly thought to be from the middle of the 19th century. The Romany gypsies used the word Chavi when they meant 'delinquent youth' (a young person

who has broken the law).

2) Some people believe that it comes from a nickname for the residents of the town of Chatham.

3) Others say it comes from Cheltenham, where the pupils at Cheltenham Ladies' College refer to undesirable boys of the town as 'Cheltenham Averages'. If you take the first two letters from that phrase you do, of course, get 'Chav'.

4) In a similar way, you can also get to 'Chav' by taking the first letters of 'Council Housed And Violent' or 'Council Housed And Vile', 'Council House Assault & Violence' and 'Council House Associated Vermin' but these are thought to have been made up by anti-Chavs, just stirring things up!

5) There are some who say that the term Chav was

used in Edinburgh, Scotland, over 15 years ago, and that the sudden popularity of the term in South-Eastern England has puzzled the people of the Scottish capital, to whom Chav is not a new term at all.

Chav was certainly the buzzword for 2004. Having wormed its way into spoken English, Chav was even entered into dictionaries for the first time. Related terms for troublemakers can be found in the dictionary entry for Chav. The popularity of these terms has grown since the 1980s, and their usage reflects both serious and light-hearted issues arising from changes in British urban life.

The act of adding unnecessary and showy modifications to something is known as Chavving Up (or Shamming Up in Ireland), and is particularly relevant if the changes are flashy but do not actually enhance the performance of the thing in question.

Indeed, most items (such as cars) that are 'chavved up' are made to look and sound 'cool' or unique in some way, but actually end up performing worse after the chavving session than they did before! This reinforces the importance of appearances in Chavworld: image is everything. It is what you are judged by.

There are other Chav-related phrases and a number of collective nouns for a group of Chavs, the most popular being a Chavalanche or a Chavalcade.

Who is the Chav stereotype or typical Chav?

A lot of people – or society in general, if you like – prefer to pigeon-hole groups or individuals. With a label it is easier for you to understand who's who and what's what. This has happened with Chavs. The Chav label was coined by outsiders (i.e. non-Chavs). Labels tend to be given to groups of people easily identified by their clothes, language, behaviour, and so forth. More often than not, labels are also given to groups of people whose behaviour is frequently interpreted as threatening or aggressive in some way. ('Lager lout' was a term once very widely used, perhaps less so now, but it brought to mind a very specific image of a certain person or group of people.)

So what is a 'typical' Chav's behaviour like? Chavs are generally considered to be loud and lower class, with 'class' describing taste, not necessarily income. Most Chavs come from not well-off, working-class families living on council estates, and get their money from the dole. The general opinion of non-Chavs is that Chavs want lots of money and possessions but don't want to have to work for it – at all, if possible.

Chavs are known for stupid, drunken behaviour and minor criminal acts, generally carried out whilst drunk (i.e. often after the pubs have closed). The many incidents reported in newspapers have only served to strengthen their bad reputation. Chavs are also known for their habit of going around in small groups, for their quickness to taken offence, and for picking fights (especially with loners).

By 'stereotype' we mean the over-simplified image of one person or group about another. The stereotype – or typical – Chav is someone who wears: brand name sports clothing and shoes (usually white trainers); fake designer clothing and accessories, particularly the distinctive pattern of Burberry; lots of 'bling! bling!' – i.e. loud, chunky, gold jewellery (especially hoop earrings for females and sovereign and signet rings for males); sports caps or hooded tops (often both are worn. The hooded tops are known as 'hoodies' and are now being banned in some shopping centres across the country); sports or jogging trousers.

Brand names are huge in Chavworld because they imply status and thus importance. The Burberry clothing brand is still very popular – specifically the baseball cap – too popular, in fact. It became so linked with the whole Chav image that Burberry stopped making it – the company didn't really want to be associated with the Chav trend! It hasn't made a difference to Chavs, though, as they can still get fake Burberry caps from Canal Street in New York,

and the Costa! Who's to know the difference?!
There is a very well known photograph of Chav
Princess Danniella Westbrook, all kitted out in
Burberry (skirt, top, hat, etc.), with the ultimate
accessory – a Burberry-clad baby and in a Burberry
patterned pram!

It has to be said that female Chavs usually overdo
it just a little on the make-up and accessories front.
They tend to plaster on far too much make-up, as
well as fake tan (so that it looks obviously fake!).
The overall look is rounded off with a hairstyle
commonly known as the Council House Facelift.
This name is unflattering but very descriptive. It
refers to the skin on the face being stretched really
tight. This is because the (usually badly-dyed and
orangey) hair is pulled back into a tight bun, pulling
on the skin.

A lot of Chavs own a large, dangerous attack dog

and a heavily adapted car (usually a Vauxhall Nova).
If a Chav doesn't have either of these things, he
is sure to be aiming to get them. They are status
symbols. Having a car and a guard dog mean that
the Chav has made it; he is somebody of importance.

Cars are definitely important as far as image goes.
A car worth any street cred must have a great music
system with amplified bass. This goes with the
enjoyment of mainstream rap music (by males) or
R&B (by females), and pop and dance music by
both sexes. The rap group Goldie Lookin' Chain
does a great send-up of the Chav ideals.

Chavs use mobile phones a lot. In fact, mobile
phones are like an extension of a Chav's body! It
doesn't matter where they are or whom they are
with, Chavs will use their phones – in cinemas and
restaurants, on the bus, etc. – without seeming to

care about anyone else.

Chavs love reality TV shows such as *Big Brother*, *Celebrity Love Island* and talk shows like *Trisha*. Many Chavs would give anything for their 15 minutes of fame on *Trisha*.

Hobbies include drinking, clubbing and sex (usually, but not necessarily, in that order).

Media portrayal

The character of Vicky Pollard, as portrayed in the BBC comedy series *Little Britain* by Matt Lucas, along with Catherine Tait's Chavette (with her catchphrase, "Am I bovvered?") are two of the best and most popular examples of a female Chav. Girls like this are often known as Kappa Slappas, after their favoured clothing brand Kappa and the word 'slapper'.

Members of the Gallagher family of the Channel 4 series *Shameless* share many Chav characteristics including alcohol abuse, petty criminality, under-age sex and caring for a large family on state benefits. In this case the family is presented in a kind light, in much the same way as you would find the sympathetic Scally characters in *Brookside* and *Boys from the Blackstuff*. As Sophie Webster once said in *Coronation Street*, 'When we grow up, me and

Chesney are going to be Chavs!'

Julie Burchill wrote a piece in *The Guardian* in 2005 defending the Chav girls. She argued that reduced social mobility means that Chavs don't put much faith in education. Chavs are more likely (and reasonably so) to think they have a better chance of making it if they take a leaf out of Jade Goody's and Victoria Beckham's books.

Celebrity Chavs

Celeb-type Chav examples are Blazin' Squad for the boys and Jordan, Jodie Marsh, *Eastenders*' Kat or Danniella Westbrook for the girls.

Prince Harry has been cited as Chav-like because of his liking for baseball caps, sportswear, drinking, and drugs, and for his links with glamour models. However, his upper-class background goes against the grain of the typical council-estate Chav. So at best Harry would have to be called a wannabe-Chav.

Our very own glamour model Jordan (otherwise known as Katie Price) is a great role model for Chavettes. She has masses of money, doesn't really do much, makes no pretence about who and what she is, has fun and doesn't take herself too seriously (the Eurovision 2005 trials and that pink outfit confirm this!).

For a certain group of Chavs, David and Victoria Beckham are particular role models. The whole Beckingham Palace ego trip, and their endless self-promotion built them up. David Beckham's alleged marital straying only seemed to make him more likeable and sympathetic. It was as if his faults made him more like one of the lads, as it were.

The footballer Wayne Rooney would fit the Chav stereotype even better. His abusive language and anti-social behaviour as depicted in the tabloid press are exactly what people think of when they hear the word 'Chav'. And he has that well-known Chavette of a girlfriend, Coleen, to spend all his well-earned cash for him. Who has ever seen her without a shopping bag?

Michael Carroll is widely regarded as representing the height of Chav culture. When the petty criminal and former dustman won the National Lottery Jackpot of over £9 million, he spent a large proportion of his winnings on gold jewellery, alcohol, drugs and cars.

The Reality Television star Jade Goody is widely regarded as a Chav role model, having had two highly publicised pregnancies and no obvious income.

Charlotte Church and Coleen McLoughlin are often each referred to as 'Queen of the Chavs' by tabloid newspapers and gossip magazines. This dubious title has been given for various reasons. Both ladies can display a huge lack of style – although it has to be said that Coleen has upped the stakes and is now appearing more and more in fashion magazines, rising in the fashion icon stakes and bringing Primark with her. They both have a tendency to get very drunk. Allegedly. They both go for laddish rich boyfriends (without the course of true love ever running smoothly). Neither shows any appreciation for the value of money (their own or anyone else's for that matter)!

Hannah Murray is a Chavette normally seen wearing sportswear, fake designer gear and large hoop earrings. She is also well known for the fur-lined Chav coat that she wears indoors!

You know you're a Chav when...

1. The only Churchill you have ever heard of is a dog who sells insurance.

2. You let your thirteen-year-old daughter smoke at the dinner table in front of her kids.

3. You've been married three times and still have the same in-laws.

4. Jack Daniels tops your list of "Most Admired People."

5. You wonder how service stations keep their toilets so clean.

6. You think that Dom Perignon is a Mafia leader.

8. You go to your family reunion looking for a date.

9. Your school disco has a crèche.

10. Your engagement and wedding rings are full sovereigns from Argos.

11. You have to go outside to get something out of the 'fridge'.

12. One of your kids was born on a pool table.

13. Your dad walks you to school because you are both pupils there.

14. You can't get married to your sweetheart because there's a law against it.

15. Your toilet paper has page numbers on it.

16. Your weekly food shopping consists mainly of baked beans, crisps and Pot Noodles.

17. Your mum cannot baby-sit because she is in the hospital giving birth.

18. The Job Centre staff gives up sending you to interviews.

19. You get followed round shopping centres by security.

20. They will not let you into Bluewater shopping centre in Kent.

21. They will let you into Lakeside shopping centre in Essex.

22. You receive a birthday card from the Job Centre and Social Services every year.

Gear

Brand, brand and nothing but brand!

Think Burberry or white Nike baseball cap, tracksuit items, Von Dutch t-shirts, spanking prison-white trainers, sovereign and signet rings and multi-layered gold white-boy-bling chains from Argos – always worn over the clothes ... no matter what the clothes are!

Chavs have such a tribal dress code that you can spot them miles away! What makes Chavs attire so funny is that they think they are at the cutting-edge of fashion and that by weighing down their body with hunks of worthless 9ct-gold rubbish they look rich! In reality most (non-Chav) people think this whole image is a very funny thing to see.

Chavettes Favourites

The Kappa brand
Stilettos
Tight tops
Short skirts
High boots
Morgan or Kookai bags
Low-slung Miss Sixty jeans.

Chavo Favourites

Football (particularly Arsenal) shirts
Berghaus or Tog 24 coats
Helly Hanson jackets.

General Favourites

Kappa
Burberry

Mera Berghaus caps
Nike hoodies
White Nike trainers (Air Max, especially)
Stripey jumpers
Sports socks with tracky bottoms tucked into them
Rockport footwear (Rockies).

Sportswear

Baseball Cap

There is a theory that all Chavs are issued with a
baseball cap at birth. It has to be said that they look
so natural together that the theory is very believable!
Chav caps are either worn at a weird angle, or back
to front, or just so as to cover up the Chav's identity
to the max! Look out for the distinctive Burberry

variety. Other favourites include: the Mera Peak
Berghaus in grey, Nike and Kappa.

Branded Shirts and Jackets

Branded sportswear and nothing but branded
sportswear: this is what the average Chav-about-
town likes to be seen wearing. The bigger the better,
as far as the brand name on the item of clothing
is concerned. (What would be the point of a tiny
name that no one would see when the whole idea is
to flaunt it?) Favourites are: Lacoste t-shirts, Fred
Perry polo shirts, England and Arsenal shirts, Henry
Lloyd jumpers and jackets, Helly Hanson jackets,
Ben Sherman shirts, Stone Island, etc.

Footwear

Most Chavs don't actually own a pair of shoes. But
they are likely to have several pairs of trainers – and

the latest styles at that! All they have are white
trainers. Like all Chav attire, a really obvious, in-
your-face name is a must! It goes without saying
that Chav trainers must be spanking clean (they are
often referred to as 'prison white') to make it look
like they are new. Reebok Classics are a favourite,
as are Rockports (Rockies), and Nike Air Max.
Timberland boots (or Timbies as they are best
known) are favoured by Scottish Chavs (Neds).

Jewellery and Accessories

Bling! is the word. This was first used in the 1990s
to describe the imaginary sound of light reflecting
off a diamond. Nowadays, to 'bling! bling!' means
to wear over-the-top, flashy, sparkly jewellery. And

Chavs sure do like to bling!

It's quantity, not quality that matters. The bigger, the better – masses of gold clanking away gives the wearer street cred, and that is all-important in Chavworld.

Remember Mr. T. from *The A-Team*? He summed up the Chav outlook when he said, all that time ago, "I believe in the Golden Rule – the man with the gold... rules." And what about the original Chav, Jimmy Saville – of the tracksuits, medallions and rings fame?! He was chavving it decades ago!

Chav bling is mostly bought from Argos or Bid TV. Failing that, Chavs can always try Lord of the Bling in Walford Market. Chav bling at the local Argos provides all the huge hoop earrings, curb chains, nametag and clown necklaces, bangles, bracelets, necklets, anklets, cufflinks, knuckledusters, rings, rings and more rings that a Chav could hope to wear all at once.

Argos won't let a Chav down on brand either, with loads to choose from: Quiksilver, Nike, Playboy, Ben Sherman, and so forth. When there's no local branch of Argos, help with diamante purchasing is at hand in the form of the Freeview TV channel, Bid TV.

Thick Gold Chains

Quantity and size definitely matter, especially where gold chains are concerned. Thick curb chains, medallion-like items and clown necklaces are really in. Usually anything between five and eight chains is worn for maximum bling-in-your-face effect.

Sovereign and signet rings

Blinging rings = rich person.

The sovereign ring was once just for cockney villains, scrap merchants and Jimmy Saville. But now the Chavs have hijacked this tasteful item for themselves. This and the diamond-studded signet ring are the ultimate bling status pieces. This status is confirmed each time the Chav in question greets one of his 'homies' (friends). The 'Yo' greeting is usually accompanied with a slack flick of the fingers, frequently very near to the friend's face. This guarantees that no diamond will go unnoticed.

Big hoop gold earrings

Chavettes will fight for the biggest hoops
going. To have any street cred the Chavette's
hoops must be at least 2 inches in diameter.
Anything less is laughable.

Watches

Jacob watches are THE things for Chavs to wear.
The real thing costs in excess of £4,000 and Chavs
will do almost anything to get one. At a pinch, a
good fake one will do.

Accessories

Accessories for Chavettes

Burberry, Morgan or Kookai handbags
(or fake ones).
Burberry umbrellas, scarves and underwear.
Brightly coloured synthetic scrunchies.
Perfume, namely: Burberry London for
Women, Burberry Tender Touch for Women,
Burberry Brit for Women, Burberry Touch for
Women, Burberry Weekend for Women.

Accessories for Chavos

An attitude.
A hard, shifty expression.
Scent: Burberry Brit for Men, Burberry
London for Men, Burberry Touch for Men, and
Burberry Weekend for Men.

Names

N.B. Some spellings and pronunciations vary, but here are some top Chav names. (Hint: 't's are often silent, so Britney becomes Bri'ney; 'th' is pronounced 'f', so Samantha becomes Samanfa, etc.)

Chavettes:

- Beyonce
- Bianca
- Britney
- Casey
- Caz
- Chantelle
- Chardonnay
- Charmaine
- Chazza
- Chelsea

Coleen

 Danielle

 Donna

 Jade

 Jordan

 Katie

 Kayla

 Leah

 Mercedes

 Michelle

 Monneye

 Natalie

 Nikkie

- Rachelle
- Samantha
- Sharon
- Shaznay
- Shell (Michelle)
- Shirley
- Stacie
- Tammy
- Tiffany
- Tracie
- Trish
- Vicky
- Waynetta

Chavos:

- Barry
- Brooklyn
- Cruz
- Darren
- Dave
- Dwayne
- Gary
- Jason
- Kevin
- Kyle

Lance

Larry

Lee

Lexus

Liam

Nathan

Nova

Rickie

Shane

Trevor

Wayne

Language

The Native Chav Lingo

Although the official language in the United
Kingdom is English, very few natives are able to
speak it fluently. Those who can usually don't
mingle with the majority of the population, but
choose instead to work in publishing or some
other poncey job like that, telling each other how
wonderful they are and how the weather is in
Tuscany and how wonderful it is that Bluewater has
banned hoodie-wearing Chavs, etc!

Here is a quick guide to learning the Chav language.

Examples of Chav lingo:

'paahh'	=	'power'
'aahh'	=	'hour'
'abaahht'	=	'about'
'gaahhing'	=	'going'
'naahthing'	=	'nothing'

Last Letters:

Try not to pronounce the last letter of a word. If you do, Chavs may get confused. This often leads to a good shoeing (kicking).

Examples:

Drop the 't' sound from 'about'.
Say 'abou' ('abaahh' is the correct pronunciation) not 'about'.
Say 'cun' not 'cunt', as in 'Up yaahh cun!'

-ing:

Never pronounce 'ing' at the end of a word. This will just make you sound like a Chinese person to a Chav. He will then either beat you up or try to order number 16 with egg fried rice. 'Ing' can be pronounced 'in', but in some circumstances becomes 'ink.'

Examples:

Say 'goin' (the correct pronunciation is 'gaahhn') not 'going'.
Say 'blazin' ('good') and 'steamin' ('drunk').
Say 'nuffink' and 'sumfink' rather than 'nothing' and 'something'.

Th / F:

Don't say 'th' when 'f' will do. Sometimes even the
'f' is not used.
Examples:
Say 'Fanks' not 'Thanks'.
Say 'naahhnk' not 'nothing'.

Double Negatives:

Use as many double negatives as you can, even
tripling and quadrupling them if you feel it will
make your feelings more clear.

Example:

Say 'I ain't never daahhn naahhnk!' rather than 'I
haven't ever done anything!'

Swearing:

Swear words can be very helpful and are used as frequently as possible. The crudeness of the language depends on how much White Lightning has been drunk or how much glue has been sniffed by the Chav in question.

'Fuck' punctuates sentences when vocabulary is lacking. It is apparently easier if 'fucking' is used to replace adjectives and 'cunt' is used to replace a person.

Swearing at the beginning of a sentence is preferable, as it makes the person you're talking to sit up and listen. If you can't manage that or simply forget, try swearing in the middle of words.

Examples:

Say 'Fucking, I was round Steve's the other day'

rather than 'I was round Steve's the other day'.
Say 'It was absofuckinglutely wicked!' as opposed to
the very boring 'It was absolutely wicked.'

General:

Use the vowel sound as often as you can, even
between words. Try to create a flowing, whining
noise as you speak. Sentences with too many
consonants can confuse a Chav. He may then pop a
pill and start raving. This will be very inconvenient
if you're trying to draw him into a discussion about
the moral implications of the Israel / Palestine
situation.

Be as nasal with your voice as possible. This is
more easily achieved if you make a conscious effort
to never open your mouth properly. No one will
understand what you're saying, but after a few
hours in typical Chav haunts you'll have nothing

interesting to say anyway.

Wave your arms around a lot and never make eye contact with the person you're talking to. Eye contact is seen as threatening behaviour and may lead to a shoeing.

Further examples of common phrases, taking into account all of the points mentioned so far, are:

'Gaahhn daahhn taahhn?' ('Are you planning a trip into town?')

'Aahhv yaahh goh?' ('Have you got?', meaning 'Do you have any?')

Here are some favourite sayings it might be worth your while learning:

'Wot u lookin at?' or 'Wot da fuck yoo lookin' at?'

('Is something the matter?')

'Wot u fuckin' say?' ('I beg your pardon?')

'Go' any fags?' ('Do you have a cigarette, please?')

'Iz minted.' ('I'm in the money.')

'Check it!' ('Look at that!')

'A righ' minger' ('A very ugly person')

'Sweet' ('All right' or 'OK')

'Nah m8.' ('No, my friend.')

'Numpty' ('Unfashionable')

'Light-weight Shady Pants' ('Someone can't take their drink')

'Alriitee / a'ight' ('OK'. Used as a greeting, often said with a swift flick of the fingers.)

'Oioi.' ('Hey.')

'Innit?' ('Isn't it?')

'S'up?' ('What's happening?')

Acronyms / Abbreviations:

TMC   (Totally Mint Condition)
TWOC   (Taken Without Owner's Consent)

And for our friends north of the border:

'Here, Wee Man... Big Malckie's gonna Kick yer ballix in, so 'e is. Ye may way watch yerself, here 'e comes nay. Do ya want me ta hold onta yer dope for ye, he loves it so 'e does. Big Malckie's only outta Hydebank an' 'e doesn't like it on the outside, 'e's lookin' da go back in. Watch yerself. Givus yer fackin dope nay.'

Translation: 'Excuse me, young man, Big Malcolm is about to physically assault you. I would be on the lookout if I were in your shoes, I can tell you. If you like, I can hold onto your marijuana for you while you get a stomping, as the aforementioned

Malcolm is partial to a bit. Malcolm has just been released from the young offenders' institute, and apparently liked it so much that he wants to return soon. As I said, look out. Hand over your marijuana immediately.'

Topics of conversation:

Football, fighting, sex, *Big Brother*, being bored, winning the Lottery, Argos catalogues, the latest Nike advert on the box, Kung Fu, *Coronation Street*, *Bad Girls*, *Footballers' Wives*, *Eastenders*, *Trisha*, sex, money, becoming rich by doing nothing, being spotted by the producer of a reality TV show and becoming famous, sex, money.

The Chav Dictionary

WELCOME to the dictionary of Chav speak. This very useful reference section will help you learn the Chav language. Yes, this growing breed of scallies, charvers and layabouts has gradually developed its own language that is completely nonsensical to the untrained ear. But read on and all will become clear!

When you have read and taken on board some of the terms used by Chavs, you may well be amazed at what a difference this will make to your life. The next time you walk past a group of Chavs outside a bowling alley, bus station or cinema, try eavesdropping – you may be surprised at what you hear.

A

alloy
noun

Term used to describe a mixture of metals, more precious to Chavs than gold. Many Chavs are known to dream about having new wheels for their Novas made from this combination of precious metals.

'ave
verb

The Chav speak abbreviation of the English 'have'. Its use in Chav English is decreasing as the term 'stealed' becomes ever more popular.

arse
noun

This should not be confused with the English

word 'ass', meaning 'donkey'. In Chav speak, 'arse' refers to the area of the body from which most Chav speak is uttered.

a'ight
expression / greeting
Used as a greeting, normally coupled with a slack jaw and a swift flick of the fingers, this is the equivalent of 'Hello. How are you?'.

aun'ie
noun
A kin-term used in Chav speak to describe the female friends of any Chav parent. From an early age Chav parents confuse their children's understanding of kin-terms by encouraging the presence of such fictitious 'aun'ies'.

B

baaastard

noun

An insult – often used when Chavs are caught out by the DSS for benefit fraud or their neighbour sends the environmental health round to their house to investigate the stench.

beauty

adjective

This is a vague term (used to replace an unpleasant or offensive term). It is now hardly ever used to refer to a person, as inbreeding has taken over in Chav communities, leading to a mass ugliness epidemic. The only current use of this adjective evident in Chav speak is when a speaker is referring to a set of recently stolen hubcaps that actually look the same as alloy wheels.

bench

noun

Objects found outside bowling alleys, cinemas, and amusement arcades in every town centre or leisure complex in the country. No true Chav can afford to enter any of these establishments, and thus is grateful to local councils for providing him with somewhere to sit and abuse the public.

bill

noun

Here is another spectre of Chav mythology. Rumour has it that bills must be paid in order to receive goods and services. However, any self-respecting Chav knows that it is more cost-effective to get rehoused than to pay up.

bo

adjective

An adjective used in Chav speak for expressing the positive qualities of any item. For emphasis it can be preceded by 'well' or 'proper'. Also refers to the smell emanating from armpits.

bollocks

noun / adjective

i) *Noun.* The male genitalia.

ii) *Adjective.* The term used to describe something as awful, particularly car stereos, stolen TVs or clothes that are unbranded.

brother

noun

i) The person any self-respecting Chavette desires to wed.

ii) A sibling of the same parents – the identity of

whom is often unknown.

bucket

noun

This refers to a cheap way for a Chav to consume 'weed'. The Chav saves on tobacco and Rizlas by adopting this D.I.Y. approach to drug consumption.

C

Chav

noun / verb

i) *Noun.* The manifested humanitarian equivalent to either stepping on an upturned plug or having chewing gum stuck to your shoe.

ii) *Verb.* To steal.

Chavette

noun

The female equivalent of a Chav except with more hair mousse, a shorter skirt and a deeper voice. Chavettes can be found in their natural habitat hanging around bus stops, shopping malls and in fast food restaurants.

cousin

noun

A person ripe for marrying. At least if they look like you, you can recognise them in a crowd and you know in advance what the kids will look like.

cunt

noun / adjective

i) *Noun*. The female genitalia.
ii) *Adjective*. Used to describe a person who impedes the smooth existence of a Chav in any

way. This may be done by simply being alive, having expensive trainers or being over 16 and not having a baby.

cushdy
adjective

An expression coined in a classic British television comedy, with origins in Cockney English. In Chav speak it is used to describe a positive event such as winning £1.00 on a scratch card or getting a new key ring for your Nova that bears the Ferrari logo.

D

---

dealer
noun

A person who supplies illegal drugs, and in doing so usually affords himself high status within Chav society. Respected and loved by Chavs and their parents everywhere.

dat

pronoun

Used in place of the English 'that'. Normally used to point out another person's property, such as any car registered later than 1984 or the stereo contained within said car. 'Dat' is mutually interchangeable with 'vat' or 'nat'.

dis

preposition

Hip-hop Chav speak for the English 'this'. Linguists argue that this is simply an example of language change in modern society. The truth, however, is that Chavs just don't talk properly.

diss

verb

A contraction of the English term 'disrespect'. 'Dissing' a Chav / Chavette is easy and will frustrate him / her greatly as he / she will not be able think fast enough to come up with a response. Some excellent 'disses' to be used on Chavs are:

• You look like your mum.

• Your signet ring isn't from Argos.

• Your dad hasn't been to prison.

• Your trainers look old.

• Why do your trainers have four stripes?

• Why can your family breathe under water and swim really fast?

(Referring to the gills and webbing that have evolved out of repeated inbreeding.)

dog

adjective / noun

  i) *Adjective.* Derogatory term. A Chav may describe his girlfriend, mother or the mother of his child as being 'dog' ugly.

  ii) *Noun.* A canine pet employed by Chavs nationwide in order to gain extra benefit from the DSS.

E

easy

adjective

  Used to describe any Chavette regarded by Chav society as being over-willing to conduct sexual relations with just about anybody.

easy now

greeting

Friendly introduction used only between Chavs.
Can be followed by many words, the choice
of which reflects the speaker's opinion of the
recipient. Examples include 'bad boy', 'gangster',
'playa' and 'soldier'.

F

fags

noun

i) People of homosexual inclination. If you are gay,
never let this fact be revealed to a Chav. He will
try to give you a shoeing because he is very much
afraid of you.

ii) Cigarettes.

father

noun

A creature out of Chav mythology, often spoken of, but never seen – what Chavs become when they die / disappear / go to prison.

fingerprint

noun

Used in place of 'signature' in Chav speak. Chavs are more commonly required to sign their name in this way than with a pen. Most Chavs cannot write anyway.

fit

adjective

Used in an unconventional sense in Chav speak as its meaning bears little resemblance to the English form. For a Chav / Chavette to call someone 'fit', the subject must be 'well frosted', have 'nuff bling' and definitely be 'phat'.

flex

noun

Most commonly used in the phrase 'What's the flex?' This has the same meaning as the English phrase 'What's going on?' Only it's not the same, because it is 'wack'.

flexing

verb

If you are 'flexing' a Chav, you are more than likely annoying him or her because to 'flex' is to insult or frustrate. 'Flexing' a Chav is easily done; just ask simple maths questions, or request that they spell something (anything) or write their own name without using just the symbol 'x'.

frosted

adjective

This word is used to describe the status of one's 'bling'. If one's bling is 'well frosted', it is assumed to be voluminous in quantity, usually meaning that you have 'nuff gold', or a signet ring wiv a real pound coin.

fuck

expletive

This English taboo word is encouraged in Chav speak and should be used regularly and with much bravado. (E.g. 'What the fuckin' fuck is fuckin' 'appenin' wiv your fuckin' bling – it was nuff frosted but now it's fuckin' wack, innit?')

G

---

gangster

noun

To be a gangster is the pinnacle of Chav ambition; it provides a career path, status, consumables and respect. Being a 'gangster' offers Chavs the chance to live an existence outside of the law – a bit like all other Chavs, really.

geek

noun

Used by Chavs as a term of respect for people more intelligent than themselves. People can qualify as a 'geek' in the eyes of a Chav in many ways. These range from knowing how to tie their own shoelaces, to wearing glasses or not smoking.

grass

verb / noun

   i) *Verb*. Used to refer to the act of reporting any crime to the police or anyone in authority.

   ii) *Noun*. This refers to the person who committed the act of 'grassing'. Being a grass almost certainly guarantees being beaten up.

   iii) *Noun*. Marijuana.

H

hat

noun

   A popular fashion accessory worn by most Chavs to conceal their identity from CCTV cameras in petrol stations, shopping centres, football stadiums and prison line-ups across the country.

I

innit

tag question

Contraction of the English 'isn't it?' An extremely
popular expression used by Chavs at the end
of 'sentences' in order to qualify their previous
statement. An example of this phenomenon is 'Dat
stereo is well phat, innit?'

J

joint

noun

The preferred method of consuming marijuana
used by Chavs. This option is only available when
tobacco and Rizlas can be afforded, usually on
benefit day.

joyride

verb

When a Chav procures another person's vehicle
with the intention of doing handbrake turns
and wheel-spins in the car park of any garden
centre or supermarket, he or she can be said
to be 'joyriding'.

K

kicking

noun

Used by Chavs in place of the English 'beating'.
'Kickings' are either given or received by Chavs. In
both instances it usually involves someone younger
than the Chav.

knob

noun

i) The male genitalia. Commonly found growing from the foreheads of most Chavs.

ii) An insult.

iii) A household fixing that must be forced in order for Chavs to successfully burgle your house.

L

---

large

adjective

In Chav speak, this adjective not only refers to the physical size of the object in question, but also defines an object as being rather good. Thus it is unlikely that however fat a Chavette gets, she will ever be 'large'.

lemon

noun

When a recently purchased Nova saloon proves to
have sawdust in the engine, no exhaust pipe and is
held together by rust, in Chav language it can be
said to be a 'lemon'.

lie

noun

The Chav speak equivalent of the English term
'truth'. 'Lies' are used by Chavs in a number of
situations such as police questioning, teacher
interrogation and paternity tests. Apparently
daytime TV diva Trisha has invented a foolproof
'lie detector test' to spot any Chav 'truths'.

life

noun

What some Chavs end up getting, courtesy of any sane-minded judge, for any combination of road-traffic offences, dole fraud or fashion crimes.

luv

noun

A sexual emotion shared between a Chav and his Nova or a Chavette and her hair mousse. Similar to the English term 'love' but spelt differently and of a more sexual orientation.

M

man

noun

Any well-constructed sentence in Chav speak should end with 'man': 'That signet is well phat, innit man?'

massive

noun

In Chav speak, unlike in English, the term 'massive' is a noun, not an adjective. Chavs are not massive. A 'massive' is something that refers to a large collection of Chavs, usually found loitering with intent around cash machines, leisure complexes and scrap-yards.

me

pronoun

Chav speak form of the English 'my'. For example 'Me trainers are well phat, innit man?!'.

microwave

noun

Item found in every Chav kitchen in the country. All meals in Chav households are prepared using this technological wonder. Apparently you put

cold food in for 30 seconds and it comes out hot
enough to melt steel. Believe.

mint
adjective

Euphemism used to describe the condition of a
recently purchased / stolen Nova saloon or Mk2
Fiesta. If said vehicle comes equipped with either
neon underlighting or blacked-out windows, it can
be said to be 'well mint'.

minger
noun

A term used to describe the more beautiful of the
Chavettes. The antonym of 'minger' is 'absolute
disgrace'. Examples of mingers in society are Posh
Spice, Jade and Jordan.

money

noun

Another legend from Chav mythology, money is thought to be 'rarer than gold' by most Chavs. Although 'money' is freely dispersed by the DSS on production of a ration book, most Chavs will never know what it is like to hold a real £20 note.

mother

noun

The first lady of the Chav household. She is often found whiling away the days watching daytime TV in her dressing gown, yelling at little Chavs, and smoking 60+ cigarettes a day. Defining characteristics are:

i) a penchant for smoking

ii) being single

iii) a love of TV-related magazines.

motor

noun

Used in Chav speak to refer to any car that has been 'enhanced' with plastic body kits, stick-on 'carbon fibre' accessories or go-faster stripes. The true Chav will always have a 'motor', whether it has an MOT or not.

N

---

naff

adjective

A dying expression favoured by Chavs in the late '90s to describe something that isn't 'mint', 'phat', 'large' or 'bo'.

nah

particle

'Nah' has the same meaning as the English 'no'.

Used most commonly as a direct response to the questions, 'Is that your baby?', 'Do you live here?' or 'Have you been in paid employment in the past 365 days?'

nick

noun / verb

i) *Noun*. Refers to the English term 'prison', a place where many Chav families have been known to spend Christmas or meet up with long lost relatives.

ii) *Verb*. To steal.

nuff

adjective

A mutated version of the English 'enough', used by Chavs in place of the English intensifier 'really'. So in Chav speak, your bling is not 'really frosted' but 'nuff frosted'.

nuffink

adverb

Can be used interchangeably in place of either
'anything' or 'nothing'. 'Nuffink' is a term usually
used by Chavs in conjunction with the verbs 'got',
'have' and 'done'.

O

open

adjective

This is an important term in Chav speak, used
as an excuse when confronted by the police, a
homeowner or an ex-girlfriend's parents.
E.g. 'The door was already open', 'The windows
were open' or 'Her legs just opened'.

P

pap
adjective

Derogatory term used to describe any object, event
or place that falls below the inflated expectations
of a Chav. An example might be 'Southend is pap'.

phat
adjective

A term used in Chav speak to describe the width
of a gold chain, the quality of a pair of new Nike
Air or the girth of a Chavette.

poor
adjective

The social status most Chavs aspire to being. It
is easily obtainable, doesn't involve work and it
ensures the DSS gives you money.

proper
adjective

An adjective to be used anywhere in a sentence to intensify another adjective. (E.g. 'My Argos gold necklace is proper phat, innit man.')

Q

quit
verb

What Chavs do after twenty minutes in any type of gainful employment.

R

razz
verb

If you drive your vehicle excessively fast around school playgrounds, market squares or car parks, then you can be said to be 'razzing' it. Chav people can also 'razz', especially when being chased by dealers, the police or the DSS.

refrigerator

noun

An upright chilling cabinet, used for keeping energy drinks cold. Classed in English as 'white goods'. For Chavs, however, the term 'stolen goods' is more appropriate.

rights

noun

Chavs tend to be read their 'rights' from a very early age, usually by policemen or parents who don't know any bedtime stories.

ruff

adjective

i) A derogatory term used to describe the physical state of Posh Spice or most Chavettes.

ii) A euphemistic term used to describe the 'phatness' of the bass levels offered by one's stereo system.

iii) The noise a dog makes.

S

safe

adjective

When a Chav breaks into your home and takes your TV, video and Playstation (items which you should have put in the safe), and manages to escape, he is truly 'safe'. (Unless the police catch his cap-wearing behind and throw him in the 'nick' with the rest of his family.)

scally

noun

Thanks to a lack of birth control, Scallies are
a growing breed of Chav, found mainly in
the North West. Their specialist skills include
burglary, abusing old people, making babies
smoke and stealing hubcaps.

skank

noun

Every Chav is a skank: someone who always wants
something for nothing and is more than prepared
to steal if needs must. The noun 'skank' is not to
be confused with the verb 'skanking' which is a
popular form of dancehall dancing.

Sharon

name

The favourite choice of most Chavettes, especially when it means naming their daughters after themselves.

sharp

adjective

A descriptive term used to describe a Chav who is wearing brand new white trainers, the latest Nickelson pastel-coloured polo shirt and freshly ironed 3-stripe tracksuit bottoms. Such an outfit would make anybody look 'sharp'.

shite

noun / adjective

i) *Noun*. Excrement.

ii) *Adjective*. Term used to describe how 'pap' something is. (E.g. 'That motor is fuckin' shite, innit man.')

shoplifting

verb

Shoplifting is the favoured hobby, or indeed job, of most Chavs. It is a route to clothing and feeding your child, prison and missing school, and is thus a highly respected activity in Chav communities.

signet

noun

Not to be confused with the term 'signature', 'signet' is a type of grotesque finger jewellery worn by the more well-to-do male Chav. If the owner is particularly wealthy it may contain a real pound coin as its centrepiece or be engraved with the word 'phat'.

sorted

adjective

When a crime is successfully carried out and a
new packet of nappies or a new signet ring is in
the sticky hands of the Chav, things are said to be
'sorted'.

shoeing

verb

The Chav speak term for 'beating somebody up'.
If a 'shoeing' is dealt out by a Chav, it will never
hurt because the soles of his shoes are always made
of air and thus soft to the touch.

squawk

sound

The high pitch vocalisation made by a Chavette,
when in mating season. This happens every
Tuesday night when the bowling alley shuts early.

T

tax

verb

To steal. This term should not be confused with
the English word 'tax', as the only 'tax' that Chavs
pay is that which the government levies on their
cigarettes. Paying income tax entails having a job
and paying council tax entails having a house.

twister

noun

Anyone who messes with the mind of a Chav
by demanding simple motor-neurone skills such
as adding, subtracting, reading or writing can
be described as a 'twister'. Most teachers are
thought to be 'twisters'. (Not to be confused
with 'twizzlers', a cherished item on most Chav
menus and made famous by Jamie Oliver's 'School

Dinners'. Even though everyone knows that this kind of food is not the most nutritious, Chav mums are still buying it in bulk for their kids.)

TMC

acronym

'TMC' stands for 'Totally Mint Condition'. The term is used to describe any rust-free Nova saloon, Fiesta or Escort XR3i.

TWOC

acronym

Taken Without Owner's Consent. Legal jargon designed to confuse simple-minded Chavs. Only found in Chav speak because of the massive numbers of Chavs that have been exposed to the term when being arrested for nicking.

TV / television
noun

The favourite possession of most Chav parents. The more committed enthusiasts, and owners of satellite dishes, can watch television for anything up to 24 hours a day. Televisions can be stolen and traded in pubs for money or wheel trims.

U

ugly
adjective

A word used to describe the facial characteristics of most Chavs and Chavettes. Unlike the story of 'The Ugly Duckling', most Chavs cannot hope to blossom into beautiful swans, although they have a similar life expectancy (at the moment this is ten years shorter than the national average).

V

vat

pronoun

Chav speak form of the English 'that'. Used
referentially by Chavs to point things out in time
and space. E.g. 'Vat motor is bling.' (Not to be
confused with anything financial whatsoever.)

W

wack

adjective

When something is 'shite', it is also, by definition,
'wack' and vice versa. Trainers that aren't white are
'wack', as are jobs, fathers, teachers and shirts that
don't bear the cross of St George.

wa g'wan

phrase

    'Wa g'wan' is a contraction of the English phrase 'What is going on?' In Chav speak it is a 'hip-hop' term of greeting.

washing machine

noun

    An item referred to in Chav mythology. Used for making your socks and England shirts whiter than white. 'Washing machines' are found in laundrettes across the country but rumour has it that soon they will be affordable enough for residential purchase.

Wayne

name

    'Wayne' is the Chav speak equivalent of the English term 'Jesus'. Chav parents name all of

their male children 'Wayne' in the hope that
they will be the next 'chosen one' and possibly
make it to the Promised Land, otherwise
known as 'college'.

well

intensifier

Used in Chav speak in place of the English
term 'really'. Anything can be 'well' good,
'well' bad, 'well' large or 'well' phat. Chavettes
are 'well' phat.

wheel-trims

noun

Objects used by Chavs as a form of currency,
to trade for various goods and services. The
advantages of using them instead of money are
that they are more easily obtainable, there is a
greater range of denominations (based around a

variety of styles) and they are big so you
can't lose them.

wiv

preposition

'Wiv' is a mutation of the English term 'with'.
When a Chavette is the girlfriend of a Chav (or is
pregnant by him), she can be said to be 'wiv' him.
It is similar in meaning to the English expression
'the partner of'.

X

Don't be ridiculous. Chav's don't know any words
beginning with 'x'.

Y

yellow newspapers
noun

Advertising newspapers which are treated as both books and catalogues by Chavs. All Christmas shopping is done with the aid of such retail bibles. Through them it is possible to obtain almost any item you can imagine for under £5.00. This includes cars.

yo
greeting

A greeting between Chavs that can be repeated as many times as the speaker wishes. In fact it might be suggested that two 'yo's' are better than one. E.g. 'Yo. Yo yo. Yo yo yo. Yo yo yo yo'.

Z

See X, although it is tempting to include the word 'Zebra', just for posterity.

Lifestyle: likes and dislikes

General

Likes	Dislikes
Maccy D's	Conran
Drinking	Being sober
Clubbing	Cocktail parties
Shagging	Drinking cocoa
Smashing Phone Boxes	Playing Scrabble
Drugs	Warm milk
Smoking	Exercising
Racing Novas	Rambling
Joyriding	Taking the tube
Getting stoned	Reading the Bible
Spitting	Cleaning teeth
Lying	Conversing
Acting hard	Empathising

Strutting	Being self-effacing
Chips and curry sauce	Salads
Football	Cricket
Arguing	Debating
Fighting	Compromising
Free travel	Season tickets
Cash	PAYE
Cadging	Working
Argos catalogues	War and Peace
The Daily Star	The Times
The Sun	The Economist
Picking on loners	Being a loner
Bwise	John Lewis
Poundstretcher	Selfridges
Mark One	Marks & Spencer
Shoefayre	Church's
Bus shelters	Coffee bars

Music

Likes

R & B
Hip-Hop
UK Garage
Dance
Happy Hardcore
New Monkey
Black Metal
After Dark
Makina
Eminem
50 Cent
Usher

Dislikes

Classical
Trad Jazz
Gothic music
Moby
Chris de Berg
Slipknot
Bauhaus
Adrift
Mozart
Val Doonigan
Ella Fitzgerald
Barry Manilow

TV

Likes

Trisha
Big Brother
Emmerdale
Eastenders
Jerry Springer
The Lottery
Footballers' Wives
Bad Girls
Coronation Street
Hollyoaks
The Simpsons
Celebrity Love Island
I'm a Celebrity, Get Me
Of Here

Dislikes

Question Time
Newsnight
Gardener's World
Changing Rooms
Parkinson
Mastermind
Morse
House
Songs of Praise
Crimewatch
Friends
News
Last of the
Summer Wine

Football Focus
Match of the Day

Test Match Special
London Marathon

Cars

Likes

Vauxhall Nova
Vauxhall Corsa
A stereo bass that
makes the car shake
Under-car neon lighting
Razzin (racing in car
parks)
Burberry seat covers
Go-faster stripes
Oversized exhaust
Black-out windows
Wheels costing over
£1,000

Dislikes

Volvo Estate
Rover 200
CD changer

Mats
Doing 30 mph

Velour upholstery
Air freshener
Nodding dog
Furry dice
Hanging
St Cristopher

Hangouts

Likes

Train stations
Off licences
Shopping centres
Street corners
Car parks
Parks
Bus shelters
Markets
Local Chippie
Macdonalds
Harvester

Dislikes

Ticket offices
Wine bars
Department stores
Offices
Connexions
Libraries
The Job Centre
Marks & Spencer
Pizza Express
Café Rouge
All Bar One

Holidays

Likes	Dislikes
Ramsgate	Eastbourne
Margate	Hove
Clacton on Sea	Yorkshire Dales
Southend	Scilly Isles
Blackpool	Tiree
Great Yarmouth	Bath
Ibiza	Egypt
Gibraltar	Sicily
Fuengiroli	Tuscany
Torremolinos	Paris
Butlins	Club 18-30
Woolwich ferry	Cross Channel ferry
Isle of Sheppey	Isle of Sky

Chavs like to go on holiday to places where they can feel secure by being with lots of fellow Chavs. The food and drink have to be British. All day breakfasts and burger and chips with a side order of pizza are best.

In this country Chavs head to Ramsgate, Margate, Clacton on Sea, Southend, Skegness and Blackpool. In these resorts they can completely relax amongst their own. God help any Goths who try to venture to these towns in the height of the season. Spotty students should steer clear too.

'Abroad' generally means one place: the Costas (Spain) have been drawing shell-suited Brits for many years now and many of them have set up homes in towns like Fuengiroli and Torremolinos. Chavs used to a diet of egg and chips will find countless cafes selling the food that they love and – as an added bonus – run by fellow Chavs! With

no need to speak any Spanish, our adventurous
Chavs have only one thing to worry about: the sun.
With no idea about sun cream Chavs soon turn a
lobster colour and many have to find their way to
the local hospital to be uncooked. Have fun sitting
in a beach bar watching your fellow countrymen and
women trying to walk when their skin is cooked and
stretched tighter than lycra round a Chavette's bum!

Food and Drink

Favourite food shops: Netto, Lidl, ASDA, Greggs (for the sausage rolls – check out the queue at lunch times!).

Favourite eating-places: Maccy D's, Burger King, Dominos Pizza.

Favourite food: Turkey Twizzlers, crisps, chips with curry sauce, Pot Noodles.

Favourite drinks: White Lightning, Thunderbird Red, MD 20/20, Buckfast, Smirnoff Ice, Bella, White Storm, Vodka & Coke, Scrumpy, Bacardi Breezers, Tennant's Super, Taboo, WKD, Pulse (with blackcurrant), Diamond White, Lambrini, Foster's, Babycham, Carling... Owt dat can git uz pissed.

Chav Dinner Party

As guests arrive serve them a glass of chilled Lambrini and take their hoodies and coats to the bedroom. Some time later go through their pockets to see if you can score some loose change. After all, you are treating them to an evening of sophisticated conversation.

MENU

Starter:

Prawn cocktail flavour crisps for the ladies and pork scratching for the men.

Main course:

Choice of mini hot dogs or Fray Bentos steak and kidney pie covered with a Pot Noodle surprise. The vegetables come in the form of chips and beans. This whole concoction is mixed into a mash by some and eaten with a big spoon without looking up once.

Suggested drink:

White Lightning or Buckfast.

Pudding:

Mars bars cut up and covered with ice cream. This mixture in turn is covered by chocolate sauce and hundreds and thousands. A truly sumptuous feast which will be the talk of the pub for a day.

Suggested dessert wine:

Thunderbird red.

Jokes

How do you start an argument with a Chav?
Speak.

What do you call a Chav in a tastefully
decorated house?
A burglar!

What do you call a Chav in a box?
Innit.

What do you call a Chav in a filing cabinet?
Sorted.

What do you call a Chav in a box with a
lock on it?
Safe.

What do you call an Eskimo Chav?
Innuinnit.

Why are Chavs like slinkies?
They have no real use but it's great to watch one fall down a flight of stairs.

What do you call a Chavette in a white tracksuit?
The bride.

What do you say to a Chav at work?
'Big Mac, please.'

How do you identify the bride at a Chav wedding?
She is the most pregnant one.

What do Chavs use as protection during sex?
The bus shelter.

'How many children?' asks the council worker.

'10,' replies the girl.

'10?' asks the council worker, 'What are their names?'

'Wayne, Wayne, Wayne, Wayne, Wayne, Wayne, Wayne, Wayne, Wayne and Wayne.'

'Doesn't that get confusing?'

'Naah...' says the girl 'it's great because if they are out playing in the street I just have to shout WAAYNE, YER DINNER'S READY! or WAAYNE GO TO BED NOW! and they all do it.'

'What if you want to speak to one individually?' says the troubled council worker.

'That's easy,' says the girl, 'I just use their surnames'.

What do you call a large group of Chavs all going to one place (like a pub)?
A Chavalanche.

If you see a Chav on a bike, why should you try not to run him over?
It might be your bike.

What's the difference between a Chav and a coconut?
One's thick and hairy; the other's a coconut.

What's the first question at a Chav quiz night?
'Wot you lookin' at?'

How do you get 100 Chavs into a phone box?
Paint three stripes on it.

Two Chavs in a car without any music.
Who's driving?
The police.

What do you call a Chav in a boiler suit?
The prisoner.

What do you call a Chav with half a brain?
Gifted.

What do you call Chavs with a brain?
A crowd.

What happens to a thought in a Chav's head?
It dies of loneliness.

What do you call a Chav in a suit?
The accused.

What do you say to a Chav in a suit?
'Will the defendant please stand?'

Why do Chavs always travel around in pairs?
One can read and one can write!

A bus full of Chavs was driving through
Wales. As they were approaching
Llanfgogogferrinfourasoch they started
arguing about the pronunciation of the town's
name. They argued back and forth until they
stopped for lunch. As they stood at the counter,
one Chav asked the blonde employee, 'Before
we order, could you settle an argument for us?
Would you please pronounce where we are...
very slowly?' – The blonde girl leaned over
the counter and said,
'Burrrrrrrr-gerrrrrrr-Kiiiiing.'

What's a Chav's favourite ice cream?
Mint.

What do you call a Chav in a dinner jacket?
Waiter!

What do you call a Chav in the dock?
Guilty.

What do you call a Chav at college?
The janitor.

Where do Chavettes go for work?
Street corners.

What do you get if you cross a Chav
with a monarch?
The royal mint!

Latest Chav quotations

Real-life Chav situations...

Enter Chav mother, pushing a pram that contains a screaming, herpes-ridden baby covered in sores.

Chav Baby: Waaaaaaaaaaaaah!

Chav Mother: That's it! I'm eatin' your fuckin happy meal.

Outside Boots on Belfast's Royal Avenue, Saturday afternoon.

Chav One: Whata fuck is youse guana dee now, here?

Chav Two: I duano. Bur me fuckin eyelids are sweatin.

In McDonald's Peckham

Chav 1: (spills a McDonald's coke on a white tracksuit top): Fuck! nah man. I just nicked dis from matalan last week innit.

Chav 2: Shit. dat woz aite n all. de bst place 2 jak em from is frm dwn market or me m8 wrks jd sport he getz me shit all time bt he dont care cuz he jus wants 2 go on dole agen. Not boverd if he gets caut cuz it dont matta anywayz ini.

A Chav in Blockbuster told her friend that she had forgotten to 'rewind the DVD'.

And presenting some classic chavisms, overheard in Surrey:

1   'Did they have guns in world war one?'
2   'Which way up is horizontal?'
3   'Do windmills actually go around?'
4   'Is Britain communist?'
5   'You get free money out of cash points so why
    are people poor?'
6   'Yeah Jewish, that's a country isn't it?'

Two Chavettes on a bus...

Chavette 1: So ha'd'you git on last night then?
Chavette 2: Yeh, great. We woz havin a snog round
            the back, like, and 'e only goes an' sticks
            hiz 'and up me skirt, innit?!
Chavette 1: 'eeee neva!
Chavette 2: For real!
Chavette 1: Sa wot you do then?
Chavette 2: Well I giz 'im a slap, innit? Sez 'Oi!
            Wherez ya fuckin manners?! It's tits
            first!'

Chav Horoscopes

We've put together these Chav horoscopes for you to enjoy.

Chav Aries Horoscope

21 March – 20 April

Chavs need no special lucky charms today. Everything you do is filled with luck. The giro you have been waiting for will arrive on time and you will have luck at the bookies.

Chav Taurus Horoscope

21 April – 21 May

Chav Taureans are very bossy. You might find yourself wanting to hog the White Lightning tonight. Don't! Share it with the girl with the huge earrings and you could be lucky too!

Chav Gemini Horoscope

22 May – 21 June

Your stars predict some bad luck coming your
way. Either your job seeker's allowance will be
withheld, pending investigation of you working
cash in hand at a car wash, or your white trainers
will accidentally step into a great pile of dog shit
without you knowing. You will only find out when
your Nova starts to smell like a shit house! Best
stay in today.

Chav Cancer Horoscope

22 June – 23 July

Your mother won't babysit for you this week so you will have to stay in and look after the kids yourself. Plan ahead and buy in some strong white cider and curry Pot Noodles so you won't miss out on getting legless.

Leo Chav Horoscope

24 July – 23 August

Lucky Leos will not spend all their giro today on alcohol as the till girl will make a mistake and not charge you for something. You will find something unexpected when you go to the pub tonight. Whatever it is do not keep it to yourself (unless it is crabs).

Chav Virgo Horoscope

24 August – 23 September

Take the family out for a meal to bring
harmony to your life. The kids will love a
Happy Meal anyway.

Chav Libra Horoscope

24 September – 23 October

The wisest of all Chavs, the Librean will succeed in making money this week. The £10 lottery win shouldn't be squandered on pork scratchings but reinvested in more scratch cards if you are to get that spoiler for the Nova. Sorted!

Chav Scorpio Horoscope

24 October – 22 November

An extra spoiler and a go-faster stripe on your
car will make you feel more in control of your life
than before. Have a large tin of beans on toast for
breakfast and use the empty tin to fashion a cool
exhaust for the motor.

Chav Sagittarius Horoscope

23 November – 21 December

Chavettes should make the most of their natural
beauty today and only wear three pairs of earrings
and one big gold-coloured chain. Also a clean pair
of thongs wouldn't go amiss girl!

Chav Capricorn Horoscope

22 December – 20 January

Your lucky number is 4 and your lucky Chinese meal is number 61. Seeing as that's Sweet and Sour Pork with a Side Order of Chips, you should be in Heaven.

Chav Aquarius Horoscope

21 January – 19 February

Watch out for men with clipboards turning up
on the doorstep. It could be the man from TV
licensing. Just say that you are the plumber and
that the owner will not be back from holiday for a
fortnight. Do not let him in.

Chav Pisces Horoscope

20 February – 20 March

Unpaid court fines will come back to haunt
you this week. If you are skint make sure you
are light on your toes as the law has a warrant
for your arrest.

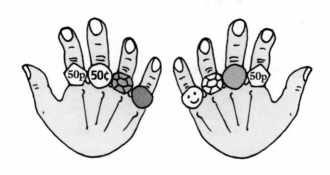

134

CHAV ICONS:
TOP 10 COUNTDOWN

CHAV ICON No.10

MR T

"I pity the fool..."

The coolest man in *The A-Team* (not so difficult),
Laurence Tureaud was born in the Southside area of
Chicago. He became a professional wrestler and tag
team partner to Hulk Hogan and was twice named
the USA's toughest bouncer ("pity the fool that
comes in here in jeans or trainers"). He was also
a bodyguard for Steve McQueen, Diana Ross and
Mohammed Ali. Since *The A-Team* was axed he has
resided in L.A. with a poodle called Mr Snuffles.
OK, so I made up that last bit. Don't tell him.

CHAV ICON No.9

ELVIS PRESLEY

Elvis Aaron Presley of East Tupelo, Mississippi, gave birth to Rock 'n' Roll and sold one billion records. No fewer than 149 gold, platinum and multi platinum records adorn Graceland. He made 31 movies, including *Jailhouse Rock* and *King Creole*.

In 1969 Elvis played 57 dates in Vegas and broke all box office records. He is the only person to be a member of three Halls of Fame: Rock 'n' Roll, Gospel, and Country.

He gave away Cadillacs, cash and jewellery, wore black and white rhinestone-studded jumpsuits, rings and scarves, and grew obese on deep fried peanut butter and banana sandwiches, and ice cream.

He once sent his personal jet to Denver for a burger. He died in his bathroom from a massive overdose of cocaine and barbiturates.

He was still topping the charts in January 2005, with a re-release of 'One Night' becoming the 1,000th No.1 single in the UK. Accept no imitations; he's the King of Bling. Thengyewvermuch. Elvis has left the building.

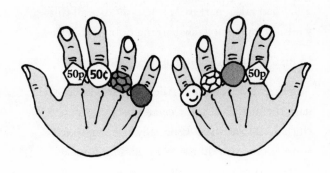

CHAV ICON No.8

SIR JIMMY SAVILLE

James Wilson Vincent Saville was a miner, bouncer and club manager before becoming the *mos def* DJ in Britain.

With his cool catchphrases – 'howsaboutthatthen' and 'eueueueueu' – he became the first and longest-lasting presenter of BBC TV's *Top of the Pops*. He presented *Jim'll Fix It* from 1971 to 1991 and by 2002 had taken part in 214 marathons – all this whilst being completely barking doolally treefrog.

In his 70s, he is the Godfather of Bling.

The rings, the tracksuits, the platinum mullet-style hair, the medallions, the cigars, the dead mother's clothes... He da man! Especially as he managed a mini-come back in the form of a *Big Brother* appearance (January 2006)!

CHAV ICON No.7

BEYONCE

Beyoncé Knowles – a founding member and chief songwriter of Destiny's Child – is one of the biggest female acts of all time, selling more than 33 million records worldwide.

In 2001 Beyoncé won the *ASCAP Pop Songwriter of the Year Award*. This made her the first African-American woman (and actually only the second woman ever) to win that award. Destiny's Child launched in 1997 with their blingin' hit, *No, No, No*. In 2001 they took home two Grammy awards.

Beyoncé has worked with artists ranging from OutKast's Big Boi to Missy Elliot, and from Jay-Z to the late Luther Vandross. Beyoncé has a burgeoning acting career, appearing as Foxy Cleopatra in *Goldmember* and, more recently, in *The Pink*

Panther. She can also be seen on the small screen in a series of commercials for Pepsi Cola directed by Spike Lee.

She advertises Star perfume and is the spokesperson for L'Oreal. Why? Because she's worth it.

Bling!

CHAV ICON No.6

VICTORIA 'POSH SPICE' BECKHAM

Gucci tabloid queen. In her teens, Posh Spice used to beg her dad not to drive her to theatre school in the Rolls Royce. She joined the Spice Girls, whose hit *Wannabe* was the first of nine to go straight to number one in the charts. In one year alone they sold 35 million albums. She met the footballer David Beckham in 1997 – a marriage made in tabloid heaven. They have three sons: Brooklyn (named after where he was conceived); Romeo; and Cruz.

When her eponymous solo album floundered she worked with Hip-Hop artists to increase her street cred. An 'A' list celeb and clothes horse who will never be seen in anything that isn't by Prada or D&G – or without a plasterer's trowel full of make-up.

She remains too skinny by half – go to Maccy's D's for a quarterpounder, girl!

CHAV ICON No.5

J-LO

Dancer, actress, and now singer – is there anything she can't do? After Lopez became a well-known actress, her early marriage to Ojani Noa came under close scrutiny by the press, and they were divorced after only a year. Her film *Anaconda* was a huge success. She also co-starred with Jack Nicholson in *Blood & Wine*, Sean Penn in *U-Turn*, and George Clooney in the critically acclaimed *Out Of Sight*.

Lopez switched her focus to music with the 1999 album *On The 6*, to which big-name, modern-day producers like her then boyfriend, Sean 'Puffy' Combs, lent a hand.

Jennifer's appearance at the Grammys in her infamous down-to-there Versace dress, and at the Oscars in a braless, see-through Grecian gown and mink-fur false eyelashes, ensured that she remained in the public eye.

Her quickie wedding to dancer Cris Judd was even shorter than her first marriage and her engagement to actor Ben Affleck. *The Wedding Planner* was the number one film in the U.S.A. the same week that her album *J.Lo* held the top spot on the *Billboard* Top 200. She launched her own clothing line, as well as a perfume (*Glow*) and an L.A. restaurant.

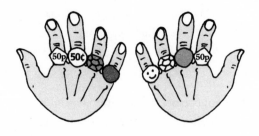

CHAV ICON No. 4

JORDAN

Jordan, real name Katie Price, is arguably Britain's best-loved glamour model, famous for her surgically enhanced breast of mammoth proportions and her ability to have her outrageous antics chronicled in the tabloids and magazines on practically a daily basis. Ex-Page 3 Sun girl and failed-Baywatch wannabe, Jordan did herself proud on *I'm a Celebrity, Get Me Out of Here*, flirting with and ending up with Peter Andre. Her bid to represent Great Britain in the 2005 Eurovision Song Contest will go down in Chav history as a totally over-the-top, unforgettable performance. Jordan remains a source of great interest to many people, as sales of her autobiographies (*Being Jordan* and *Jordan: A Whole New World*) have proved. A larger than life and well-loved Chav icon!

CHAV ICON No. 3

COLEEN MCLOUGHLIN

Coleen has helped the Chav fashion industry no end, with her all-over velour pink tracksuits, over-sized blinging gold jewellery, spanking white trainers, designer-like bags, etc.

Coleen's shopping habit lifts her to the highest of all Chav status rankings, particularly as she gets to spend someone else's money! It has to be said that she has made herself a celebrity in her own right, regularly featuring in the tabloids and in magazines, arranging expensive photoshoots for herself as a way of filling the time. She even has her own column in the celebrity magazine *Closer*, called Welcome To My World, and a fitness DVD.

CHAV ICON No. 2

CHARLOTTE CHURCH

Charlotte Church: the original cherubic schoolgirl who wowed audiences with her classical singing has turned into the ultimate Chav party animal. Charlotte can allegedly down an impressive 10 double vodkas on an average night out on the lash. Cheeky Vimto is her favourite tipple and WKD Blue also goes down well. On her 19th birthday she went on a massive bender, admitting she can't half 'sink 'em'. The tabloids had a field day speculating about a photo Charlotte supposedly sent her boyfriend – of her topless. Although Charlotte apparently insists she was wearing a bra. Chain-smoking, vodka-swilling, attention-grabbing, whatever people call her, she's definitely a very popular Chav icon.

CHAV ICON No. 1

MICHAEL CARROLL, the KING OF CHAVS

With the nickname 'Lotto Lout', this young Chav was guaranteed big coverage in the tabloids. A former dustman, he scooped £9.7 million on the lottery but failed miserably to make positive changes to his life. Despite his good fortune, he has faced various charges ranging from drug possession to drunk and disorderly conduct and a nine-month prison sentence for affray. He has allegedly made his neighbours' lives a misery with his anti-social behaviour. This has included causing a nuisance with noise, holding late-night car races in his field, and burning a mobile home on a bonfire at a party he gave at his Norfolk home.

With his now well-known one-fingered signal (usually to reporters or anyone in authority), Michael Carroll is considered an example of a bad

Chav role model by some. But many Chavs find him – with his bad behaviour, stroppy attitude, love of bling and obvious disrespect for authority – a good laugh! He is the self-styled King of Chavs, and was quoted in *The Sun* in June 2005 as saying, 'It's good to be king'. If anyone is in any doubt, he has a t-shirt and a car sticker with the wording 'King of Chavs' just to ram home his point!

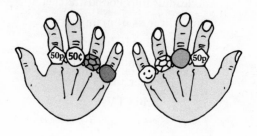

THE CHAV PRAYER

Our Giro who art in Job Centre
Chav Chav be thy name
Thy Nike come
Thy Dolce & Gabbana be done
In Burberry as it is in Iceland
Give us this day our jobseeker's allowance
And forgive us our max-outs
As we forgive those who shop against us
And lead us into Poundstretcher
But deliver us from imitation
For thine is 24 carat
The Lidl and the Argos
For ever and ever
Bid TV

All Crombie Jardine books are available from your
High Street bookshops, Amazon,
Littlehampton Book Services, or
Bookpost (P.O.Box 29, Douglas,
Isle of Man, IM99 1BQ.
tel: 01624 677 237,
email: bookshop@enterprise.net.
(Free postage and packing within the UK).

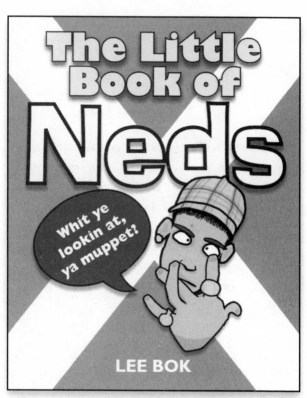

The Little Book of
Neds

Whit ye lookin at, ya muppet?

LEE BOK

1-905102-30-5 • £2.99

1-905102-73-9 • £2.99

The Little Book of

Book of

Wanking

The definitive guide to man's ultimate relief

DICK PALMER

1-905102-00-3 • £2.99

1-905102-21-6 • £2.99

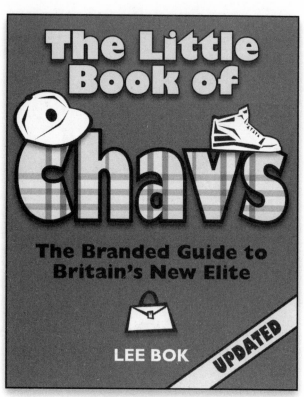

The Little Book of Chavs

The Branded Guide to Britain's New Elite

LEE BOK

UPDATED

1-905102-01-1 • £4.99

The Little Book of

GOTHS

Dan Vice

1-905102-24-0 • £2.99

1-905102-75-5 • £2.99

THE LITTLE BOOK OF
ASBOs

Asbolent behaviour from around the country

ED WEST

1-905102-41-0 • £2.99

www.crombiejardine.com